You got this
Mama

Child Birth is one of the many things

your body was built to do.

Believe in yourself.

You can do this.

Breathe.

I am ____ weeks pregnant

All of the

strength

I need is

inside of

me

I am ____ weeks pregnant

I Look
Forward
to my
Baby's
Birth

I am ____ weeks pregnant

Loose Jaw
Open Hands
Still mind

I am ____ weeks pregnant

Breathe

I am ____ weeks pregnant

each
WAVE
has a
PURPOSE

I am ____ weeks pregnant

My
BODY
was meant
to do
THIS

I am ____ weeks pregnant

I am safe
my baby is
SAFE

I am ____ weeks pregnant

I am the
BEST MUM
for my
BABY

I am ____ weeks pregnant

I am ____ weeks pregnant

I am
STRONG

I am ____ weeks pregnant

my baby's size

is **perfect**

for my body

I am ____ weeks pregnant

I GREW
This Baby
I
CAN BIRTH
This Baby

I am ____ weeks pregnant

My Mind Quiets

I am ____ weeks pregnant

I
BELIEVE
in my
BODY

I am ____ weeks pregnant

My
Body will
PROTECT My
BABY on it's
journey to ME

I am ____ weeks pregnant

My body is
STRONG
and
CAPABLE

I am ____ weeks pregnant

I am
FOCUSED
on my
CALM
and
GENTLE
birth

I am ____ weeks pregnant

My baby
moves
down
smoothly

I am ____ weeks pregnant

My body has created a miracle

I am ____ weeks pregnant

My body is
STRONG

My mind is
FOCUSSED

I am ____ weeks pregnant

I FEEL

positive

confident

&

optimistic

I am ____ weeks pregnant

I am powerful

I am ____ weeks pregnant

On the other
side of this
pain
I will
meet my
baby

I am ____ weeks pregnant

Breathe in
Relaxation
Breathe out
Tension

I am ____ weeks pregnant

There is nothing to fear

I am ____ weeks pregnant

I Am Worthy of

this Pregnancy

I am ____ weeks pregnant

I won't be afraid
I trust the process

I am ____ weeks pregnant

I am ____ weeks pregnant

I AM

AMAZING

I am ____ weeks pregnant

My job is to relax and let birth happen

I am ____ weeks pregnant

my baby
and I
are working
together

I am ____ weeks pregnant

My Body
Is Strong
And
Capable

I am ____ weeks pregnant

I breathe
in
power
I breathe
out
fear

I am ____ weeks pregnant

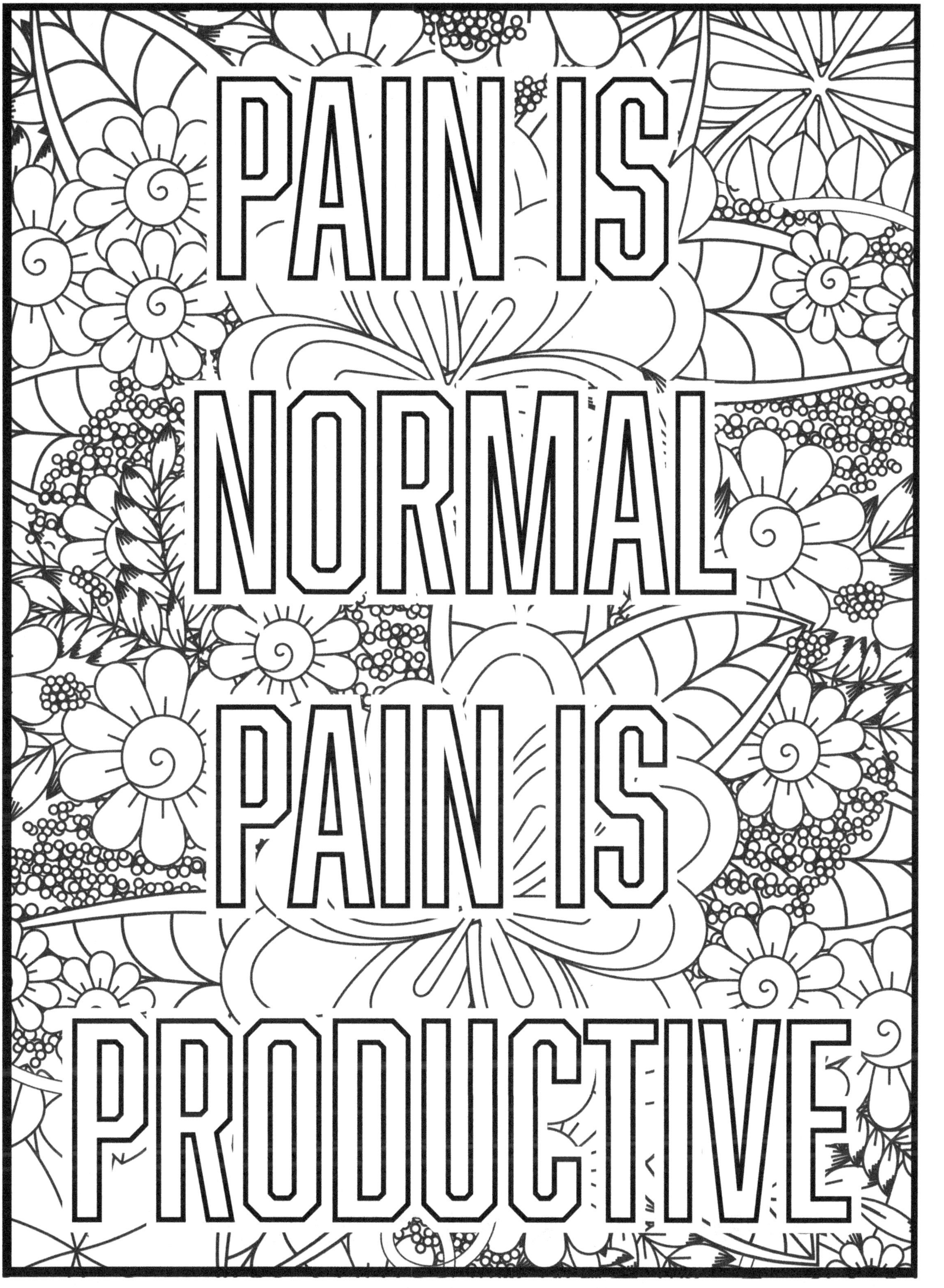
PAIN IS
NORMAL
PAIN IS
PRODUCTIVE

I am ____ weeks pregnant

My body was

Made for this

I am ____ weeks pregnant

Ride
the
Wave

I am ____ weeks pregnant

I can do anything
for 60 seconds

I am ____ weeks pregnant

The more I
relax
the more
my body
opens and
expands

I am ____ weeks pregnant

I am ____ weeks pregnant

I was
made
to do this

I am ____ weeks pregnant

RELAX.
BREATHE.
Open.

I am ____ weeks pregnant

I am fully
supported
Happy and
relaxed

Made in the USA
Columbia, SC
26 July 2025

61040429R00050